Vibe Coding for the Rest of Us

A Step-by-Step Guide for Total Beginners Who Want to Build Real Apps for Real Life

Patricia A. Farrell, Ph.D.

Book cover photo: Getty Images For Unsplash+

Amazon author page for https://tinyurl.com/yc3vff2n

The Pocket Companion Series contains:

When Your Mind Won't Stop

After the Loss: Finding Your Way Through Grief

You Are Enough: Rebuilding Your Self-Worth

At the Crossroads: Making Decisions When Nothing Feels Clear

When People Hurt: Navigating Difficult Relationships

When You Feel Stuck: Finding Movement in Hard Times

Books by Patricia A. Farrell, Ph.D.

Better Together, Book 3: Reasons we heal

The Belief Effect, Book 2: Reasons we heal

Wired for Good, Book 1: Reasons we heal

Get Out! A shrink's guide to using the great outdoors for therapy

When You Can't Pour From an Empty Glass: CBT Skills for Exhausted Caregivers

The Little Book on Learning Big Critical Thinking Skills

The Smart Kid's Survival Guide: Making Good Choices in a Confusing World

How to Be Your Own Therapist

It's Not All in Your Head: Anxiety, Depression, Mood Swings and Multiple Sclerosis

Unfiltered: Beneath the noise of our thoughts lies the true narrative of our minds

Unfiltered Again: A behind-the-scenes look at healthcare, medicine and mental health

A Social Security Disability Psychological Claims Handbook: A simple guide to understanding your SSD claim for psychological impairments and unraveling the maze of decision-making

A Social Security Disability Psychological Claims Guidebook for Children's Benefits

The Disability Accessible US Parks in All 50 States: A Comprehensive Guide

Birding in the US NOW!: A birding guide for individuals with disabilities

Contents

Chapter 1: Welcome, You Belong Here

If you have picked up this book, there's a good chance you have felt it, too. Everyone around you seems to be talking about artificial intelligence. The news says it is changing everything it is taking away, not only people's jobs, but entire industries. The dire predictions are extremely upsetting to everyone, even those whose jobs will be secure because they are in industries that are needed and where AI cannot go or will go only as an adjunct helper. The talk is from your grandkids, your coworkers, and even your neighbor down the street is suddenly building things on their computers that look like magic. And somewhere in the back of your mind, a small voice says that isn't for me. I never learned to code. I am not a computer person. I would not know where to start. That little voice is not telling you the truth, but that's understandable because everything we've ever heard about computers has been complex, requires lots of education and math, and a particular type of genius that most of us don't possess.

You can let that voice rest now. This book was written for you, and only for you. Not for computer science students. Not for software engineers. It's for the person who has *never written a line of code in their life and never wanted to*. That person can still build a real, working app this week. This chapter tells you how and why you can trust that promise. You are about to have an experience that will ignite a spark in terms of computer literacy in your mind, and you will be surprised. Yes, you will.

You Do Not Need Any of This

Before we go one page further, let's clear the table. Here is a short list of ***things you do not need*** in order to use this book:

A background in computers, coding, or technology

Math skills beyond simple addition

A college degree of any kind

Expensive software or a powerful computer

Anyone's permission

What you do need is *a computer or tablet with an internet connection, an email address*, and *a little bit of curiosity*. That is the whole list. If you have those three things, you are already qualified.

What This Book Calls "Vibe Coding"

Here is the simplest way to say it. "Vibe coding" means describing what you want *in plain, everyday words* and letting an AI program write the computer ***code for you***. You don't type the code. You don't need to understand the code. You just describe your idea the way you would describe it to a helpful friend, and the AI builds it in front of your eyes.

I'm not joking or stretching the truth in any way, because this is exactly what will happen.

The person who gave this idea its name is Andrej Karpathy, a well-known computer scientist who helped build some of the most important AI systems in the world, including work at *Tesla* and at *OpenAI*, the company behind *ChatGPT*. In early 2026, and before that in 2025, he described a new way of working where you "fully give in to the vibes" and *let the AI handle the typing while you focus on the idea.* That is where the name comes from. It caught on because it captured something real: for the first time, building software could feel less like solving a math problem and more like having a conversation.

"There's a new kind of coding I call vibe coding, where you fully give in to the vibes, embrace exponentials, and forget that the code even exists."

From Andrej Karpathy, computer scientist and co-founder of OpenAI

Karpathy was talking about his experience as an expert. But the tools he was describing turned out to work just as well, and in some ways better, for people who have never coded at all. That is the door this book is walking you through; you will decide how far that journey through that door will take you, but this is the beginning.

Why Now, and Why You

For most of computing history, building an app meant learning a programming language first. That could take months or years. It kept a lot of good ideas locked inside people's heads simply because they never learned the technical side. *Vibe coding removes that barrier.* The AI already knows the programming languages. What it needs from you is a clearly described idea and a willingness to try something, review the result, and request changes until it's right. That's right. All you have to do is say what you want. Nothing more.

That means the skill you actually need is not typing code, but knowing what you want and being able to describe it. It involves *knowing what you want* and being *able to describe it*. **You already have that skill.** You use it every day when you explain a recipe to a friend, describe a problem to a repair person, or tell someone exactly how you like your coffee. This book will show you how to point that same skill at a computer.

What You Will Build

This guide isn't a book of theory. By the last page, *you will have built six real, working apps*, using only *free tools*, with *no coding* experience required. Here is what is waiting for you in each of the chapters ahead:

1. A personal budget tracker to keep an eye on your money
2. A daily habit tracker to help you build routines that stick
3. A family calendar and chore chart to keep your household organized
4. A recipe box and meal planner for the meals you cook again and again
5. A gratitude journal for a few quiet minutes each day
6. A home inventory app, as a bonus, to keep track of your belongings

Each one is a real tool you can use on your computer, for your life, starting the week you build it.

How This Book Works

This book has ten chapters, and you should *read them in order.* The first four chapters *give you the foundation*: what vibe coding is, which *free programs to use*, and *how to describe what you want* so the AI understands you. Chapters five through nine walk you through *building each of the six apps*, one at a time, with *the exact words you can type and a clear list of steps.* Chapter ten shows you *what to do when something doesn't work* the first time, which is normal, and *where to go when you're ready for more.*

WATCH OUT FOR

Mix-ups or mistakes, explained in plain words, are noted so you can avoid or fix them in seconds.

There is no test at the end. There is no grade. The only measure of success in this book is whether you end up with an app you actually use.

A Word About Mistakes

You will make what looks like a mistake at some point while reading this book. That is not a sign you are doing it wrong. It is simply part of how this process works, for beginners and experts alike. The AI will sometimes build something that is a little off from what you pictured. *The fix is almost always the same*: you tell it, in plain words, what's different from what you wanted, and *it tries* again. One of the wonderful things about vibe coding is that the *AI will never become exhausted,* it won't tire out and will *never tell you it is refusing to revise* what it has done and what you have now asked for. **There is no wrong way to ask.** There is **no way to break your computer by trying**. The apps you build in this book run safely, in their space, and **cannot damage your files or your device.** Of course, this is one of the concerns that stops people from trying things like vibe coding. They are afraid that they are going to ruin or in some way damage their computer, and they will be responsible for this tragedy. Not so.

People Like You Who Have Done This

It helps to picture a few real kinds of readers this book was written for, because you are probably a lot like one of them. Consider someone we will call Margaret, sixty-eight years old, who spent her career as a school secretary and has never once thought of herself as a technology person. She picked up vibe coding to build a simple medication schedule for herself and her husband and now checks it every morning. Consider David, fifty-two, a retired truck driver who wanted a way to track his fuel costs and built his first app on a tablet at his kitchen table, one plain English sentence at a time. Consider Rosa, forty-five, a mother of three who built the family chore chart you will build in Chapter 7, mostly to settle arguments about whose turn it was to take out the trash or help with the dishes or some other task.

None of these people learned to code. None of them needed to. They needed exactly what you have right now: a computer, a free account, and a willingness to describe what they wanted and to try again if the first attempt was not quite right. That is the entire qualification for this book, and you already meet it.

What a Realistic First Week Looks Like

It's worth being honest about *the shape of a normal first week* so you know what to expect and don't mistake the normal bumps for a sign you are doing something wrong.

Day one usually involves *creating your free account* and building your very first small app, often the budget tracker from Chapter 5. It rarely comes out perfect on the first try, and that's expected.

Somewhere around day two or three, you will likely hit a moment when the app does something you didn't ask for or does not do something you did ask for. *This is the single most normal moment in the entire process*, and Chapter 4 and Chapter 10 both show you exactly what to type to fix it.

By the end of the first week, most beginners have one or two apps they are actually using and a growing sense that the process is far less mysterious than they expected. I know it's difficult to imagine that by the end of the first week you could have one or two apps that **you have built** and that are fully functioning for you

Nobody in this book's examples became an expert overnight, and you don't need to, either. You only need to keep describing what you want, one sentence at a time. If there is one word to keep in mind, it is "persistence." There may be times when you will want to give up, walk away, throw this book down on the floor, and ask yourself why you ever attempted this. If you feel like that, you can throw the book on the floor, take some time out, and after you've cooled down, come back to it. You will be glad you did come back.

Before You Turn the Page

Take a moment and check that you have these three things ready:

A computer or tablet with an internet connection

An email address you can use to create free accounts

About thirty minutes of quiet time when you are ready to try Chapter 5

That is everything. **You don't need to be ready to code because, basically, you are not going to** code. You are going to do something you never thought you would, and you are going to be a success at it. You don't need to feel confident yet. You just need to **keep reading**. Turn the page, and let's talk about what vibe coding really looks like once you sit down and try it.

Chapter 2: What Is Vibe Coding, Really?

In Chapter 1, you got the short version. Now let's slow down and look at vibe coding more closely, so you understand not just what to do, but why it works. Understanding the why will make you more comfortable and more confident every time you sit down to build something new.

The Old Way, in Plain Words

For decades, building software meant learning a programming language, which is a strict, exact set of words and symbols that a computer can follow. A single misplaced comma could stop a whole program from working. I know what that's like because when I was in graduate school, they gave us a free five-day course in programming, but it was Fortran, which is the science programming language, or used to be, anyway. I can't tell you how many times I wrote that simple code, sent it to the printer, and got a message that the code didn't run. It left me sitting at my console in tears until a friend came over and helped. Learning to code well could take years of study. That is the picture most people carry in their heads when they hear the word coding, and it is exactly the picture that keeps so many capable, smart people from ever trying. Vibe coding is nothing like that.

Here is the good news. That picture is no longer the only way in. A new kind of tool, called a large language model (LLM), changed the equation.

What a Large Language Model Actually Is

You do not need to remember this term, but it helps to understand it once so it stops feeling like jargon. A large language model, often called *an AI or a chatbot*, is a computer program that has been trained on an enormous amount of writing (books, articles, professional papers, etc.) and computer code. Because of that training, *it can read a plain English sentence*, understand what you are asking for, and produce working computer code that matches your request. *Claude and ChatGPT* are two well-known examples. Think of it less like a calculator and more like an extremely well-read assistant who happens to also know how to write software and who is available to you for free any time of day or night. Computers are always waiting for your input. They don't go to sleep, and they are awake 24 hours a day, seven days a week. There's always a time when they're ready for you.

When you use one of these tools to build an app by describing it in plain words, that is vibe coding. You describe the idea. The AI writes the code. You look at what it made, and you ask for changes until it matches what is in your head. Yes, it really is that simple.

Where the Name Came From

As we mentioned in Chapter 1, the term "vibe coding" was coined by Andrej Karpathy, a computer scientist who has worked at the very center of the AI world, including senior roles at Tesla and OpenAI. In February 2025, he posted a short message describing a new style of working: instead of carefully typing and checking every line of code himself, he found himself simply describing what he wanted out loud or in a chat window and accepting the AI's work, correcting it only when something looked wrong.

The name spread quickly because it named something real that many people were already feeling. It also gave permission. If one of the most respected engineers in the AI field was comfortable working this way, then a total beginner could feel comfortable trying it, too.

An Important Distinction: Vibe Coding vs. Careless Coding

Simon Willison, another well-known and widely respected software engineer who writes extensively about AI tools, has been careful to point out that vibe coding is not the same thing as being careless. His view is worth remembering as you work through this book:

"If an LLM wrote every line of your code, but you've reviewed, tested, and understood it all, that's not vibe coding in my book, that's using an LLM ***as a typing assistant.****"*

From Simon Willison, software engineer and creator of Django and Datasette

In other words, real vibe coding *still involves you* but not in the way it would have in the past. You are not stepping away and hoping for the best. You are describing your idea, watching what gets built, trying it out, and speaking up when something is not right. That ***loop, describe, watch, try, and adjust*** is the whole method. It works whether you are Andrej Karpathy or a total beginner picking up your very first AI tool this afternoon.

Why a Beginner Is Actually in a Good Spot

It might surprise you to hear this, but starting from zero *has a real advantage.* Experienced programmers sometimes fight the process, wanting to control every detail the way they would if they were typing the code themselves. *A beginner has no old habits to unlearn.* You can simply describe what you want, in your own words, the way you would describe it to someone, and let the tool do its job. Willison himself has pointed out that a beginner exploring these tools for the first time gets to see, with fresh eyes, just how much is now possible *with plain language alone.*

This Is Not a Fringe Idea Anymore

It is fair to wonder whether the phenomenon is a passing trend. It is not. Serious, experienced voices in the software world have taken vibe coding seriously enough to write entire books about it for professional teams. Gene Kim, a bestselling author known for his books on how modern companies build software, and Steve Yegge, a veteran engineer who has worked at major technology companies, co-wrote a full book on the subject for working software teams, and it won a major industry book award in 2026. If people with decades of professional coding experience are studying and writing about this approach for their teams, you can feel confident that the skills you are learning in this book *are not a novelty.* They are part of how people are genuinely building software right now. This is the future of programming, and it is going to take off like a rocket, and you will be part of it.

What Happens Behind the Screen, in Plain Words

Here is *the simple version* of what happens each time you use one of the tools in this book:

1. You type a description of what you want, in plain English, into a chat box. The AI may even ask, "What can I do for you today?"
2. The AI reads your description and writes the computer code needed to make it happen.
3. The tool shows you the result right away, often as a working screen you can click on and try.
4. You look at it. If something is off, you type into the chat box what you would like changed, again in plain English.
5. The AI updates the code and shows you the new result.
6. You repeat steps four and five until the app matches what you pictured. The AI will revise as many times as you wish.

That is the entire loop. There is no separate step where you have to learn to read or write code yourself. You are always speaking in plain language, and the tool is always translating that into working software.

What a "Sandbox" Means, and Why It Matters to You

One word you may see as you explore these tools is "*sandbox.*" It simply means *a safe, closed-off space where the app you are building can run and be tested* without any chance of it affecting your computer, your files, or your personal information. Simon Willison has specifically praised this approach for beginners, noting that tools built this way let you experiment freely because the code is boxed in, cannot reach outside files, and cannot connect to other websites without your say-so. You will find, as you progress, that the AI will *ask you for permission* to do something or to open a file.

In practical terms for you, this means *there is no real way to break anything while you follow this book*. Every app you build lives safely inside the tool you are using. You are always free to try again.

I can remember a time when people were afraid to touch electric typewriters because they thought they would do something wrong. The issue was that the typewriter was so sensitive to touch that it was easy to make mistakes on the paper. The old-fashioned manual typewriters required a lot of effort, and as a result, fewer mistakes were made. They also slowed things down because an excellent typist might be able to hit 100wpm, but that would be an unusual feat. The genius Isaac Asimov, who during his lifetime wrote over 150 books, once told me that he typed over 100wpm and he never edited anything. First drafts went out to the publisher because he refused to make changes. That was Isaac Asimov, but now we understand the value of what is known as "failures."

I've said it before, and I'll repeat myself here: *there is no such thing as a "failure."* Anything you try and don't succeed at on the first attempt is one step toward success, rather than something proving that you can't do it. That's not the case. If you change your view of "failures," you're going to stick to a goal that you have set rather than putting yourself down and delivering a blow to your self-esteem. If you want to put something down and walk away for a while, or do something else because you've become frustrated with the task you are trying to do right now, that's okay. Walk away, have a drink of water or a cup of coffee, go sit on the porch or look out the window, or do whatever. Come back when you're ready.

Myths, Busted

Let's clear away a few more worries before moving on, in plain terms:

Myth: I need to understand computer code to do this. *Truth*: You will never be asked to write or even read a line of code in this book.

Myth: I need a powerful, expensive computer. *Truth*: Any computer or tablet from the last several years that can open a web browser is enough.

Myth: If I get it wrong, I could damage my computer. *Truth*: The tools in this book run in a safe, closed space and cannot harm your device.

Myth: This method is just a shortcut for people who are too lazy to learn to code properly. *Truth*: Respected, veteran software professionals use and write about this exact approach today.

Myth: I am too old, or too far behind, to pick this up. *Truth*: The entire method was designed around plain language. If you can describe an idea in a sentence, you have the only skill this requires.

How This Compares to Learning to Code the Old Way

It's worth spelling out the comparison directly, because it explains why this book can promise real results in a short amount of time. Learning traditional programming usually means studying a specific language, such as Python or JavaScript, learning its exact rules for spelling and punctuation, and practicing for months before you can build something as simple as a checklist. None of that is wrong, and some readers of this book may go on to learn traditional coding later, out of curiosity or for a career. But it's a genuinely different path from the one in this book.

Vibe coding skips the language study entirely. The AI already knows every rule of punctuation and structure. Your job is only to describe the result you want, clearly, and to recognize whether what comes back matches your idea. That is a much shorter distance to travel, and it is why a total beginner can go from zero to a working app *in a single sitting.*

A Few Honest Questions Beginners Ask

Will the AI judge me for asking simple questions or for not knowing the right words?

No. The AI has no memory of feeling impatient, no opinion about whether your question is basic, and no capacity to be annoyed. You can ask it to explain the same thing five different ways, and it will happily try a sixth. The AI may even apologize for misunderstanding what you said. While that may sound like a contradiction, it is actually a part of its internal program, and it has learned that etiquette is important.

What if I ask for something and it is technically impossible?

This is rare for the kinds of personal apps in this book. If it does happen, the AI will typically explain, in plain words, why it cannot do exactly that and suggest something close that will work instead.

Do I need to know which company made the best AI tool?

No. Chapter 3 covers several strong, free options. Any one of them is more than capable of building every app in this book. The differences between them matter far less than simply getting started with one.

What Comes Next

Now that you understand what vibe coding is and why it works, it's time to get your tools in place. Chapter 3 introduces the free programs you will use to build every app in this book, walks you through creating an account for each, and helps you decide which one to start with. *Nothing to buy, nothing to install in a complicated way.* Just a few minutes of setup, and you will be ready to build.

Chapter 3: Your Free Toolbox

A Quick Side by Side Look

A comparison of the free tools from Chapter 3: Your Free Toolbox.

Tool	Cost	Best For	Learning Curve
Claude	Free tier	Describing an app in chat and seeing it work right away	Easiest
ChatGPT	Free tier	General questions plus building simple apps	Easiest
Replit	Free tier	Apps you want to keep running and share with a link	Easy
Bolt.new	Free daily credits	Fast, polished prototypes	Easy
Lovable	Free monthly credits	Full apps with sign in and saved data	Moderate

AI programs comparison

You now know what vibe coding is and why it works. Before you build your first app, you need a place to build it. This chapter introduces the free tools this book uses, explains what each one is good at, and walks you through creating a free account. *None of these require a credit card to get started,* and none of them require you to install anything complicated. If you can create an email account, you can create one of these accounts.

What an AI Coding Assistant Is

Every tool in this chapter is what people call *an AI coding assistant*, or *an AI app builder*. In plain words, it is a website where you type what you want in a chat box, and the website's AI writes the software and shows it to you, usually within seconds. You do not download anything to your computer. You do not install any special program. You simply open a web browser, the same one you already use to check email or read the news, and go to a website. In later books, you may see that you can download a desktop version of some AI programs such as Claude, but that's not necessary now.

The One Rule for This Chapter: Pick One and Start

It is tempting to want to compare every tool carefully before choosing. *Resist that urge*. What you may actually be doing is procrastinating in the name of trying programs out, but it is anxiety that is driving it. Every tool below can build the apps in this book. The single best choice for a first-timer is the one you open first. This chapter *recommends Claude as your starting point,* because it lets you describe an app and watch it appear as a working screen in the very same window where you are chatting, with nothing extra to set up. But if you already have an account with one of the others, that is a perfectly good place to begin, too.

One additional word of advice here: ***always save everything you build***. Whenever you are done with something, tell the AI to save it, and ask where it is going to be saved, or give it a place to save the app you have created. ***Never fail to do this.***

Claude

Claude, made by a company called *Anthropic*, is a general-purpose AI assistant that also happens to be excellent at building small apps. When you describe an app inside Claude, it can show you a working, clickable version right inside the conversation, using a feature called *Artifacts*. You can click buttons, type into boxes, and try the app immediately, then tell Claude in plain words what you would like changed.

Simon Willison, the software engineer we mentioned in Chapter 2, has specifically pointed to this feature as an ideal starting point for complete beginners, because the app runs in a safe, closed space where it can't affect your computer or files, and it cannot connect out to other websites unless you allow it. See that one word, "allow"? Yes, many times the AI will ask you to allow it to do something. It will not do it on its own.

Creating a Free Claude Account

1. Open your web browser and go to claude.ai

2. Choose the option to sign up, and enter your email address, or continue with a Google account if you prefer

3. Check your email for a confirmation code or link, and follow the instructions to confirm your account

4. Once you are signed in, you will see an empty chat box. That is where you will type everything (i.e., your prompts) in this book

ChatGPT

ChatGPT, made by *OpenAI,* is probably the AI tool you have heard the most about. It works in a similar way to Claude: you describe what you want in plain English, and it can write and show you code. Its free tier is a fine place to build the apps in this book if you already have an OpenAI account or if you simply prefer its style of conversation.

Creating a Free ChatGPT Account

1. Open your web browser and go to chatgpt.com

2. Choose to sign up with an email address or an existing Google or Microsoft account

3. Confirm your account through the email or code you receive

4. Once signed in, you will see a chat box at the bottom of the screen, ready for your first message

Replit

Replit is a good choice once you want an app that keeps running on the internet so you can open it from your phone or share a link with a family member. Replit's AI feature, called *Agent,* can build an entire small app from a plain English description and can also test the app itself before showing it to you. Replit's free tier is a great way to learn, and its paid plans are only necessary if you outgrow the free daily limits. I know right now you are probably thinking, "How will I possibly outgrow the free daily limits?" You may very well do that, and you will surprise yourself when and if you do.

Creating a Free Replit Account

1. Open your web browser and go to replit.com

2. Choose "Sign Up" and create an account with your email or a Google account

3. Once signed in, look for a button that says "Create" or "Create App."

4. Choose the option to describe your app in plain English, or *look for the Agent feature*

Bolt.new

Bolt.new is built for speed. Type a description, and within moments you will see a working preview of an app you can click through. It is a strong option when you want to see results as quickly as possible. Its free tier gives you a daily allowance of building credits, which is more than enough to work through the projects in this book a little at a time.

Creating a Free Bolt.new Account

1. Open your web browser and go to bolt.new

2. Sign up using your email address or a Google account

3. You will land directly on a chat box labeled with something like "What do you want to build?"

4. Type your description there to get started

Lovable

Lovable is designed for people who are not professional developers and want to build a complete app, including features like saved data and user accounts, without touching any code. It gives you a set number of free credits each month, which is enough to build and refine the projects in this book, especially if you spread your building sessions out.

Creating a Free Lovable Account

1. Open your web browser and go to lovable.dev
2. Sign up with your email address or a Google account
3. You will see a prompt box on the main screen asking what you would like to build
4. Type your app description directly into that box

A Quick Look

A Quick Side by Side Look

A comparison of the free tools from Chapter 3: Your Free Toolbox.

Tool	Cost	Best For	Learning Curve
Claude	Free tier	Describing an app in chat and seeing it work right away	Easiest
ChatGPT	Free tier	General questions plus building simple apps	Easiest
Replit	Free tier	Apps you want to keep running and share with a link	Easy
Bolt.new	Free daily credits	Fast, polished prototypes	Easy
Lovable	Free monthly credits	Full apps with sign-in and saved data	Moderate

Note: *Claude has three different tiers*, and you will most probably use the second tier, which is CoWork. It's pretty much the same as regular Claude, which is primarily for chat mode and requesting things.

Which One Should You Pick?

If you are not sure where to start, use this simple guide:

If you want the simplest possible way to try an idea in the next five minutes, *start with Claude.*

If you already use ChatGPT for other things and feel comfortable there, stick with ChatGPT.

If you know you will want to *check your app from your phone or share it* with someone else right away, start with Replit.

If you want to see a finished-looking preview as fast as possible, try Bolt.new.

If your app idea involves saved logins or multiple people using it, Lovable is built for that from the start.

Every app in this book can be built using any of these five tools. The instructions in Chapters 5 through 9 are written to work no matter which one you chose. When a step looks a little different depending on your tool, this book will tell you so.

What Happens When a Free Tier Runs Out

Free plans are genuinely free, but most of them *place a daily or monthly limit* on how much you can build before you need to wait or consider a paid plan. This is not a trick. It simply reflects the real computing cost of running these tools. For the purposes of this book, here is what to expect and how to work around it comfortably:

If you hit a daily limit, the tool will usually tell you plainly and let you know when it resets, often the next day. But some tools, like Claude, may reset in five hours if you have a Pro plan.

You can spread the projects in this book *across several days* instead of building everything in one sitting. There is no rush and no benefit to hurrying.

If one tool's free limit is too tight for your pace, it costs nothing to create a free account with a second tool and switch between them. Yes, you can have several free accounts with different AI programs. Nobody said you couldn't.

None of the apps in this book require a paid plan to build or to use on an ongoing basis.

A Word About Privacy

WATCH OUT FOR

Never type real passwords, full bank account numbers, medical details, or your Social Security number into any AI chat box, even for a practice app. Use made-up, placeholder information instead. It works exactly the same for learning purposes and keeps your real information safe.

You Are Ready

Pick one tool from this chapter, create your free account, and keep the tab open. In Chapter 4, you will learn exactly how to describe what you want so the AI understands you the first time and what to do when it does not. Then, in Chapter 5, you will build your very first app.

Chapter 4: How to Talk to AI So It Builds What You Want

You have your tool. You have your free account. Now comes the single most useful skill in this entire book, and it has nothing to do with computers. It is the skill of describing what you want clearly enough that another person, or in this case an AI, can picture it, too. This chapter teaches you a simple formula for doing exactly that.

What a Prompt Is

A *prompt* is simply the message you type to the AI. That is the whole definition. There is no special format, no required punctuation, and no penalty for writing it the way you would naturally speak. If you can describe your morning routine to a friend, *you already know how to write a prompt.*

The Four-Part Prompt Formula

When beginners get a result that does not match what they pictured, it is almost always because the first description (the prompt) left something out, not because they did anything wrong. This simple four-part formula fixes that by reminding you what to include. Every strong prompt in this book touches on these four things:

1. What the app is for. One sentence describing its purpose.
2. Who will use it. Usually this will simply be you or you and your family.
3. What it should do, step by step. List the actions someone will take when they open it.
4. What it should look like. Consider colors, mood, or simple comparisons, such as clean and simple or warm and friendly.

Here is a *fill-in-the-blank* version you can *reuse for any app idea*, including ones not covered in this book:

TYPE THIS PROMPT

Build me a simple app that helps me [what the app is for]. It will be used by [who will use it]. When I open it, I should be able to [first thing it does], [second thing it does], and [third thing it does]. Please make it look [style or mood] easy to read with text and large buttons.

A Weak Prompt vs. A Strong Prompt

Here is what happens when a prompt skips the formula. A **weak prompt** might simply say, "*Make me a to-do list app.*" That *could produce almost anything*. It might be plain and gray or covered in features you never wanted. It is not wrong to start this way, but it usually takes several extra rounds of back and forth to land somewhere you like.

A strong prompt, using the formula, looks more like this:

TYPE THIS PROMPT

Build me a simple to-do list app that helps me keep track of errands during the week. It will be used just by me. When I open it, I should be able to type in a new errand and add it to the list, check a box next to an errand once it is done, and clear away the finished errands with one button. Please make it look clean and simple, with large text and a soft blue color.

Notice that the second prompt is not more technical. It does not use any special words. *It is simply more complete*, in the same way that giving a friend more detail about a gift you want makes it more likely they pick the right one.

Vibe Coding Is a Conversation, Not a Single Ask

Here is something worth remembering before you build your first app: you are *almost never going to get a perfect result from your very first prompt, and that is completely normal,* even for experienced professionals. Remember what I said about "failures?" The real method is to describe your idea, look at what comes back, and then simply say what you would like different, in plain words. A few examples of what that follow-up message might sound like:

Make the buttons bigger, I want to be able to tap them easily
Change the color from blue to green
Move the add button to the top of the screen instead of the bottom
Add a place to type a due date next to each errand
That is close, but can you make the finished items show with a line through the text instead of disappearing?

Each one of those is a complete, valid message. You are not expected to know the right words in advance. You are simply *reacting to what you see*, the same way you would tell a hair stylist to take a little more off the sides.

A Few Words to Know

This book promised no jargon, and it is keeping that promise. But there are a small handful of everyday words that will come up, so here they are, explained once, in plain language:

App: a program on your computer or phone that does one job well, like tracking your budget or your habits.

Prompt: the message you type to the AI describing what you want.

Interface, or screen: the part of the app you actually see and click on.

Save or export: keeping a copy of your app or its information so it does not disappear when you close the window.

Bug: a small mistake in how the app behaves, easily fixed by describing the problem to the AI in plain words.

What to Do the Moment Something Looks Wrong

You do not need to diagnose the problem yourself. You only need to describe what you are seeing, compared to what you expected. A simple, effective message looks like this:

TYPE THIS PROMPT

This is not quite right. I expected the button to add my errand to the list, but instead nothing happens when I click it. Can you fix that?

That single sentence is enough for the AI to find and fix the issue in almost every case. Chapter 10 goes much deeper into troubleshooting, but this simple pattern, describing what you expected versus what happened, will solve the large majority of problems you run into throughout this book.

Common Beginner Prompt Mistakes, and Easy Fixes

A few patterns show up again and again with first-time users. *None of them are serious*, and all of them are *easy to fix* once you know to look for them.

Mistake one: asking for too much in a single prompt.

Trying to describe five features at once in your very first message can produce a confusing result, simply because there is a lot *for the AI to guess about*. It usually works better to *describe the core idea first*, get a working starting point, and then add features one at a time using follow-up prompts, the same way you saw in the four-part formula.

Mistake two: being vague about what you actually want to see.

A message like "*Make it better*" doesn't give the AI much to work with, because "better" could mean a dozen different things. It works much better to say exactly what you want changed, such as making the text larger or moving this button to the top.

Mistake three: assuming you have to get it right the first time.

New builders sometimes feel they have failed if their first prompt does not produce a finished app. In reality, a first prompt is meant to be a starting point, not a finished product. Every app in this book is built through several rounds of description and adjustment, not one perfect sentence.

Mistake four: forgetting to say what the app is for.

It can feel obvious to you why you want an app, so it is tempting to skip that part and jump straight to features. But the AI can't read your mind, and a short sentence about the purpose, such as "*This helps me track my daily water intake,*" often shapes the whole result in a more useful direction.

Try It Yourself, Right Now

TRY THIS

Before moving on to Chapter 5, open your AI tool and ***write one practice prompt*** *using the four-part formula for any small app idea of your own. It does not need to be perfect. It does not even need to be an idea from this book. The goal is simply to feel what it is like to describe something and watch it appear.*

WATCH OUT FOR

Don't worry about sounding technical or getting the wording exactly right. Plain, everyday language works better than stiff or formal language. Write your prompt the way you would say it out loud to a helpful neighbor.

You Are Ready to Build

You now have everything you need: an understanding of what vibe coding is, a free tool with an account ready to go, and a simple formula for describing what you want. You might want to *print that four-point formula out* on an index card or piece of paper and keep it next to your computer. Every time you are going to write a prompt, you can refer to it and make sure you hit all the correct points. Chapter 5 puts all of it to work by building your very first real app, *a personal budget tracker*, from the very first prompt to a finished tool you can start using today.

Chapter 5: Build a Personal Budget Tracker

Money worries get lighter the moment you can actually see where your money is going. That is the entire idea behind this first app. You are going to *build a simple, personal budget tracker,* a tool that lets you type in your income and your expenses and instantly see what is left over. This is your very first app, so this chapter walks through every step slowly and completely. Later chapters will move a little faster, because you will already know the pattern.

A Real-Life Example

Before you start typing, picture David from Chapter 1, the retired truck driver who wanted a simple way to see where his pension and savings were going each month. He had tried a paper ledger for years but kept forgetting to update it. His first prompt looked almost exactly like the one you are about to send. Within a few minutes, he had a screen showing his monthly income, his expenses sorted into categories, and a number at the top telling him exactly how much was left. He told his daughter it was the first time in years he actually looked forward to checking his numbers instead of dreading it.

What You Will Build

By the end of this chapter, you will have a working app on your screen that lets you:

Type in your income for the month

Add expenses one at a time, each with a short name and an amount

Sort or label each expense with a simple category, like housing, food, or fun

See a running total of what you have left over, updated automatically

This approach is the same basic idea behind many paid budgeting apps, except *you are building it yourself, for free,* shaped exactly the way you want it.

Before You Start

Open the free tool you set up in Chapter 3. This chapter's instructions *focus on Claude,* since its ***Artifacts*** feature shows you a working app instantly inside the chat. If you are using a different tool, everything still applies. You will simply see your app appear as a preview window or a link instead of directly inside the chat.

Step 1: Write Your First Prompt

Type the following prompt ***exactly as written***, or adjust the small details, like category names, to fit your life. Notice how it follows the four-part formula from Chapter 4: *what it's for, who uses it, what it* *should do, and what it should look like.* One thing to remember is that you can keep this prompt anywhere on your computer that you choose and come back to use it whenever you need it. You can also give the prompt to a friend who can use it with their Claude account.

TYPE THIS PROMPT

Build me a simple personal budget tracker app. It will be used just by me, on my own computer. When I open it, I should be able to type in my total income for the month at the top. Below that, I should be able to add expenses one at a time, each with a short name, a dollar amount, and a category like Housing, Food, Transportation, or Fun. As I add expenses, show a running total of how much I have spent so far and a clear number showing how much of my income is left. Please make it look clean and calm, with a soft green color, large readable text, and simple buttons.

Send that message (*Claude has a small arrow that you can hit or you hit "return" on your computer*), and wait a few seconds. Your AI tool will respond with a working app, *ready for you to try.* Yes, you may hesitate and think you're going to do something terrible to your computer, but you won't! Follow the prompts, do as instructed by Claude, and things will be OK. If there are any issues, they can be fixed. You can always ask questions, and the AI will answer them promptly and give you guidance that you may ask for. Of that you can be sure.

Think back to whenever you were learning something, like how to drive a car with a stick shift or even an automatic or simply to keep the car straight once you have it moving. Remember how anxious you were and how you couldn't stop the car from stalling or shift gears without grinding them? That was only at the very beginning. After that, you accomplished that task and became skillful. It's the same thing here. With practice, you will gain confidence and more skill.

Step 2: Look at What You Got

You should now see a simple screen with a place to enter your income, a form to add an expense, and a growing list of expenses below it, along with a total. It will not look identical every time, since the AI makes its own small design choices, but the core pieces should all be there.

WATCH OUT FOR

If your app is missing a piece, like the running total, *do not start over*. Simply type a message such as "*Can you add a running total at the top that updates automatically*?" and it will be added to the app you already have. You've already got the "wheel." Stop trying to rebuild it.

Step 3: Try It Out

Now try out the app with a few sample numbers to see how it works:

1. Type in a sample monthly income, such as $3000
2. Add an expense named Rent, with an amount of $1200, in the Housing category
3. Add a second expense named Groceries, with an amount of $250, in the Food category
4. Check that the running total and the amount left over both update correctly

If everything updated the way you expected, congratulations. You just built your first working app using nothing but plain English.

Step 4: Make It Yours

A budget tracker is personal, so let's shape it around your actual life. Here are a few prompts you can send next, ***one at a time,*** to customize the app further. Try any that sound useful to you:

TYPE THIS PROMPT

Can you add a pie chart or simple bar chart that shows how much I am spending in each category?

TYPE THIS PROMPT

Can you let me mark an expense as recurring, so I do not have to type it in again next month?

TYPE THIS PROMPT

Can you change the categories to Housing, Food, Transportation, Insurance, and Savings to match how I actually organize my money?

TYPE THIS PROMPT

Can you add a small note at the top that turns red if my expenses go over my income?

TYPE THIS PROMPT

Can you make the text and buttons a little larger so they are easier to read?

Each of these is optional. *Add only the features that make the app more useful for your life*, and skip the rest.

Saving Your Work

Whatever tool you used, your app stays available in your account's history, so you can return to the same conversation later and keep improving it. If your tool *offers a way to save, publish, or export the app*, such as a share link or a download option, this is a **good time to use it**, so you always have a way back to your budget tracker even if you start a new conversation for your next app. If you are not sure where that option is in your specific tool, simply ask the AI directly, for example, " ***How do I save or come back to this app later***?" and *it will walk you through the exact steps for that tool.*

If Something Goes Wrong

Here are a few common hiccups and their plain language fixes (type them without quotation marks):

The running total does not update. Tell the AI, "The total is not updating when I add an expense. Can you fix that?"

The numbers show too many decimal places or look messy. Tell the AI, "Can you format all the money amounts to look like normal dollars with two decimal places?"

You want to remove an expense you added by mistake. Tell the AI, " *Can you add a small delete button next to each expense so I can remove one if I made a mistake?"*

You will notice a pattern here that will carry through the rest of this book. Every fix starts the same way: *describe what you see, describe what you wanted instead, and* ***ask for the change.***

A Few Questions About This App

Should I include every single expense, down to the smallest purchase?

Only if that level of detail is useful to you. Many people get the most value from tracking the larger, recurring categories, like rent, groceries, phone, gasoline, and utilities, without logging every single small purchase. Start broad, and add more detail later if you want it.

Can this app replace my bank's own budgeting tools?

It can complement them nicely. Your bank's tools are built around your actual transactions, while this app is built entirely around your categories and your own way of thinking about your money, which many people find easier to actually stick with.

What if my income changes from month to month?

Simply type in your new income total at the start of each month. If you would like the app to remember past months automatically, try the prompt, "*Can you let me save a separate budget for each month so I can look back at past months?"*

Chapter Recap

You built a working budget tracker using a single, complete prompt.

You tested it with *sample numbers* to confirm it works.

You customized it with at least *one follow-up request.*

You know *how to fix* the most common small issues yourself.

One app down, five to go. In Chapter 6, *you will build a daily habit tracker*, a simple tool to help you build routines that actually stick, using the exact same method you just practiced.

Chapter 6: Build a Daily Habit Tracker

Small routines, done consistently, tend to matter more than big, dramatic changes. Drinking more water, taking a short walk, calling a family member, and taking medication on time. A habit tracker is simply a place to check off these small promises to yourself, day by day, so you can see your progress build up over time. It's also a great way to motivate yourself or to get a little push to stay involved in healthful activities and social events. Psychologists tell us all the time that we need to do simple things like this, and here is a great app to help you do it in your life. In this chapter, you will build one from scratch, and by now the process will already feel a little familiar.

A Real-Life Example

Remember Margaret from Chapter 1, the retired school secretary, and her medication schedule. Most people of a certain age take anywhere from four to six medications a day. Keeping track can be an incredible chore, and it's best not left to memory alone. After Margaret built that first app, she went back the following week and built a second one, a simple habit tracker to remind herself and her husband to take a short walk together after dinner. She said the streak counter, which shows the number of days you have completed, was what kept them going on evenings when they didn't feel like it. Neither of them had ever considered themselves to be app people. *They just wanted a nudge*, and now they had one, built in their own words.

What You Will Build

A short list of habits you choose yourself, such as Drink Water, Take a Walk, Read for Ten Minutes

A simple checkbox next to each habit for every day of the week

A way to see your streak, meaning how many days in a row you have kept a habit going

A clean, encouraging look, since this app is meant to feel like a friendly nudge, not another chore

Step 1: Write Your First Prompt

TYPE THIS PROMPT

Build me a simple daily habit tracker app. It will be used just by me, on my own computer. I should be able to type in a list of habits I want to track, such as Drink Water, Take a Walk, and Read for Ten Minutes. For each habit, show a row of seven

checkboxes, one for each day of the week. Let me check off a day once I complete that habit. Next to each habit, show a small streak counter that counts how many days in a row I have checked it off. Please make it look warm and encouraging, with a soft yellow or orange color and large, friendly text.

Step 2: Look at What You Got

You should see a short list where you can type in your habits, with a row of checkboxes next to each one. As you click a checkbox, the day should mark itself as done, and the streak counter should update. If your streak counter is not appearing yet, that is a perfectly normal first result, and *the next step shows you exactly what to say to fix it.*

WATCH OUT FOR

If the streak counter *is missing or is not counting correctly*, simply say, "*The streak counter is not working right. Can you make it count how many days in a row I have checked off in a row, ending today?*" That single sentence is enough for the AI to fix the logic.

Step 3: Try It Out

1. Type in three habits you actually want to build or keep, using your own words
2. Check off today for each of the three habits

3. Check off yesterday as well, for one of them, to see the streak counter climb to two

4. Leave one habit unchecked for today, and confirm its streak resets or pauses the way you would expect

Step 4: Make It Yours

Habit trackers work best when they match your own life. *Try any of these follow-up prompts:*

TYPE THIS PROMPT

Can you let me add a new habit whenever I want, using a small add button, instead of only at the start?

TYPE THIS PROMPT

Can you add a short encouraging message that appears once I check off all my habits for the day, like "Great job today?"

TYPE THIS PROMPT

Can you change the week to start on Monday instead of Sunday?

TYPE THIS PROMPT

Can you add a way to remove a habit I am no longer tracking?

TYPE THIS PROMPT

Can you show my longest ever streak next to my current streak, so I can see my personal best?

Saving Your Work

As with your budget tracker in Chapter 5, your habit tracker stays saved in your account's conversation history. Return to that same conversation any time *you want to keep refining it,* or ask your tool directly *how to save or share it* if you want a more permanent copy.

If Something Goes Wrong

A checkbox doesn't stay checked after you click elsewhere. Say, *"My checkboxes are not staying checked. Can you fix that so they remember my choices?"*

The habit list resets every time you reopen it. Say, "*Can you make sure my habits and checked days are saved so they do not disappear when I come back?*"

You want to see more than seven days at once. Say, "*Can you show two weeks at a time instead of just one?*"

A Few Questions About This App

How many habits should I track at once?

Most people do best starting with *two or three habits*, rather than a long list. You can always add more later with the "make it yours" prompt from this chapter once the first few feel steady.

What if I miss a day? Does that ruin everything?

Not at all. A missed day simply pauses or resets that one streak, and you begin again the next day. The purpose of the streak counter is *encouragement, not punishment,* and missing a day is a completely normal part of building any real habit.

Can I track habits for someone else, like a child, instead of myself?

Yes. Simply describe that when you write your prompt, for example, " *This app will help my child track their own chores and habits,*" and the AI will shape the wording and style accordingly.

Chapter Recap

You built a habit tracker with your own personal list of habits

You tested the streak counter with real check-ins.

You customized the app to fit the way you actually want to use it

Two apps built, four to go. Chapter 7 *turns to something many households juggle every single week,* keeping everyone's schedule and chores straight, with a family calendar and chore chart you will build next.

Chapter 7: Build a Family Calendar and Chore Chart

Anyone who has ever run a household knows the particular chaos of trying to keep everyone's schedule and chores straight using sticky notes, a shared memory, and hope. This chapter builds a simple family calendar and chore chart, a single shared view of who is doing what, and when. It is *one of the most requested kinds of app* among first-time builders because almost every household can use one right away.

A Real-Life Example

This is the app Rosa from Chapter 1 built, the mother of three tired of settling arguments about whose turn it was to take out the trash. She built it on a Sunday evening, sitting at the kitchen table with her laptop, and had all three kids' names and chores entered before bedtime. She told a friend that the biggest change was not the app itself, it was that the kids stopped arguing with her about it since the chart, not Mom, was now the one keeping score.

What You Will Build

A weekly view with a column for each day

A place to list chores and assign them to a family member's name

A way to check off a chore once it is finished

A simple, friendly look that works for every member of the household, including kids

Step 1: Write Your First Prompt

TYPE THIS PROMPT

Build me a simple family calendar and chore chart app. It will be used by everyone in my household. When I open it, I should see a weekly view with a column for each day, Monday through Sunday. I should be able to add a chore, type in who it is assigned to, and pick which day it is due. Each chore should have a checkbox to mark it done. Please make it look bright and friendly, easy for both adults and kids to read, with clear day labels at the top of each column.

Step 2: Look at What You Got

You should see seven columns, one for each day, with a way to add a new chore and assign it to a name. As chores are added, they should appear under the correct day. Clicking the checkbox should mark a chore as complete, often with a visual change like a line through the text or a change in color.

WATCH OUT FOR

If the days of the week are not lined up the way you expect, or the app assumes the week starts on the wrong day for your household, simply say, "*Can you change the week to start on Sunday, or Monday,*" whichever you prefer, and the AI will adjust it.

Step 3: Try It Out

1. Add a chore called Take Out Trash, assigned to a family member, due on Tuesday
2. Add a second chore called Feed the Dog, assigned to someone else, due every day this week
3. Check off one of the chores and confirm it visually shows as complete
4. Look across the whole week at a glance and confirm it is easy to read who is doing what

Step 4: Make It Yours

A family calendar works best when it matches how your household actually runs. Try these next:

TYPE THIS PROMPT

Can you add a different color for each family member's name, so it is easy to tell at a glance whose chores are whose?

TYPE THIS PROMPT

Can you add a way to mark a chore as repeating every week, so I do not have to add it again next week?

TYPE THIS PROMPT

Can you add a small section at the top for family events or appointments, separate from the daily chores?

TYPE THIS PROMPT

Can you make the finished chores move to the bottom of the list instead of just changing color, so the unfinished ones are easier to spot?

TYPE THIS PROMPT

Can you add a simple weekly summary at the bottom showing how many chores each person completed?

Saving Your Work

Since this app is meant to be seen by the whole household, now is a good time to check whether your tool *offers a share link* or a way to *open the app on more than one device*. If you are not sure, ask your AI tool directly, "*How can my family see and use this app on their own phones or* computers?" and it will explain the options available for the tool you chose.

If Something Goes Wrong

A chore appears under the wrong day. Say, "*The chore I added for Tuesday is showing up under Wednesday. Can you fix that*?"

You want to remove a chore you added by mistake. Say, "*Can you add a small delete button next to each chore?*"

The text is too small for younger kids to read easily. Say, "*Can you make the text and checkboxes bigger throughout the app?*"

A Few Questions About This App

What if my family does not all use the same kind of device?

That's fine. Since this is a web app, it can typically be *opened on a phone, a tablet, or a computer*, regardless of brand, as long as each device has a web browser. *Ask your tool directly* about the best way to share access across different devices.

Should young children be able to check off their chores?

Many families find that a good idea, since it builds a sense of ownership. If you want extra simplicity for younger kids, try the prompt: " *Can you use pictures or icons next to each chore instead of only text to make it easier for young children to use?"*

Can the app handle more than one household, like a co-parenting schedule?

Yes, *describe that directly in your prompt*, for example, "*This will be used across two households to coordinate a shared custody schedule*," and the AI will shape the app around that specific need.

Chapter Recap

You built a shared weekly calendar and chore chart

You tested it by adding and completing sample chores

You customized it to fit how your household actually runs

Three apps down, three to go. In Chapter 8, you will build something almost every home cook wants, *a recipe box and meal planner* to keep your favorite meals organized in one place.

Chapter 8: Build a Recipe Box and Meal Planner

Most of us cook the same twenty or so meals on rotation, yet somehow still end up staring into the refrigerator at six in the evening asking what should we eat. This chapter builds a recipe box to store your go to meals in one place, plus a simple weekly meal planner to decide ahead of time what you are making, so that six o'clock question answers itself.

A Real Life Example

One reader who tested an early version of this chapter described herself as the family's designated cook for thirty years, with a shoebox of index cards to show for it. She used this exact prompt to build a digital version of that shoebox in an afternoon, then spent a few evenings typing in her favorites while watching television. She said the moment that sold her was when she asked the app to automatically build a grocery list from the week's planned meals, something her index cards had never been able to do.

What You Will Build

A place to save recipes, each with a name, a list of ingredients, and simple instructions

A way to search or browse your saved recipes

A weekly meal planner where you assign a saved recipe to each day

A clean, simple look that is easy to read even with messy cooking hands nearby

Step 1: Write Your First Prompt

TYPE THIS PROMPT

Build me a simple recipe box and weekly meal planner app. It will be used just by me and my family on our own computer. I should be able to add a new recipe with a name, a list of ingredients, and short cooking instructions. I should be able to see all my saved recipes in a list and click on one to see its full details. Below that, show a weekly meal planner with a slot for each day of the week, where I can pick one of my saved recipes to plan for that day. Please make it look warm and homey, with a cream or light orange color and easy-to-read text.

Step 2: Look at What You Got

You should see a form to add a new recipe, a list of your saved recipes, and a separate weekly planner section below or beside it. Clicking a saved recipe should show its full ingredients and instructions. The weekly planner should let you choose one of your saved recipes for each day.

WATCH OUT FOR

If clicking on a recipe doesn't show its full details, say, "*When I click on a recipe in the list, nothing happens, can you make it open and show the full ingredients and instructions?*"

Step 3: Try It Out

1. Add a recipe you actually make often, with its real ingredients and steps
2. Add a second, simpler recipe, such as a quick breakfast or snack
3. Assign one of your two recipes to a day in the weekly planner
4. Click on a saved recipe in the list to confirm its full details display correctly

Step 4: Make It Yours

A recipe box becomes far more useful once it fits your own kitchen habits. Try these:

TYPE THIS PROMPT

Can you add a way to tag each recipe as breakfast, lunch, dinner, or snack, and let me filter my list by that tag?

TYPE THIS PROMPT

Can you automatically create a combined grocery list from whatever recipes I have planned for the week?

TYPE THIS PROMPT

Can you add a small note field on each recipe where I can write things like "my mother-in-law's version" or "add extra garlic"?

TYPE THIS PROMPT

Can you let me mark a recipe as a favorite and show favorites at the top of the list?

TYPE THIS PROMPT

Can you add a search box at the top so I can quickly find a recipe by name or ingredient?

Saving Your Work

As your recipe collection grows, it is worth checking that your tool is actually keeping your saved recipes between visits. Test this by *closing the app and reopening the same conversation*. If your recipes are gone, ask your AI tool directly, "*Can you make sure my recipes are saved and do not disappear when I come* back?" and it will set that up correctly for the tool you are using.

If Something Goes Wrong

A recipe you added is missing an ingredient or step. Simply edit it by saying, "*Can you let me edit a recipe after I have already saved it?*"

The weekly planner does not remember your choices after closing the app. Say, "*My meal plan resets every time I come back. Can you make it save my choices?*"

The list gets too long to scroll through easily. Say, "*Can you add a way to sort my recipes alphabetically or by tag?*"

A Few Questions About This App

Do I need to type in exact measurements for every ingredient?

Only as precisely as you actually cook. Many home recipes are written with approximate amounts, like a splash of this or a handful of that, and this app will happily store your recipes exactly the way you naturally write them.

Can I add a photo of the finished dish?

Some tools support adding images to an app like this. Try the prompt, "*Can you let me add a photo to each recipe*?" and your AI tool will let you know whether that is supported and how to do it.

What about recipes passed down in the family, in someone else's handwriting?

This is a wonderful use for this app. Simply type in the recipe as it was written, including any personal notes or quirks, and consider it a small act of preservation, not just meal planning. If the app does allow you to add photos, you might be able to take a photo of the original recipe, handwritten, and attach it.

Chapter Recap

You built a recipe box that stores your own real recipes

You built a weekly meal planner connected to those saved recipes

You customized the app around how your own kitchen actually works

Four apps built, two to go. Chapter 9 slows things down with *a gratitude journal,* a quiet, personal app for a few minutes of reflection each day, plus a *bonus home inventory app* to help you keep track of your belongings.

Chapter 9: Build a Gratitude Journal, Plus a Bonus Home Inventory App

This chapter gives you two apps for the effort of one, since by now you have the whole method down. The first is *a gratitude journal,* a quiet, personal space to jot down a few good things from your day. The second is a bonus project, *a home inventory app,* a simple record of your belongings that can be a genuine help if you ever need to file an insurance claim.

A Real-Life Example

A widower in his seventies who worked through an early draft of this book built the gratitude journal a few months after losing his wife, mostly at his daughter's suggestion. He was skeptical at first, expecting it to feel like homework. Instead, he said, it became the one part of his evening that felt like a conversation with himself. He built the home inventory app a week later, for a far more practical reason, after a neighbor's house fire made him realize he had no record of what he actually owned.

Part One: A Gratitude Journal

Research on well-being consistently points to one simple, low-cost habit that helps people feel a bit better over time: regularly noticing and writing down good things, *even small ones.* This app gives that habit a home.

What You Will Build

A place to type in a few things you are grateful for each day

A date stamp on each entry, so you can look back later

A simple way to scroll through past entries

A calm, gentle look suited to a few quiet minutes

Step 1: Write Your First Prompt

TYPE THIS PROMPT

Build me a simple gratitude journal app. I will use it just on my own computer. Each day, I should be able to type in a few things

I am grateful for and save the entry with today's date attached automatically. I should be able to scroll back through my past entries, with the most recent at the top. Please make it look calm and gentle, with a soft lavender or pale blue color, and simple, uncluttered text.

Step 2: Look at What You Got and Try It Out

1. Type a short entry with two or three things you are grateful for today
2. Save the entry and confirm today's date appears with it
3. Add a second entry to see it appear above or below the first, in date order
4. Scroll through both entries to confirm you can read your past reflections easily

Make It Yours

TYPE THIS PROMPT

Can you add a gentle prompt or question each day, like, what made you smile today, to help me get started writing?

TYPE THIS PROMPT

Can you let me look back at entries from a specific month, instead of scrolling through everything?

TYPE THIS PROMPT

Can you add a soft background image or simple pattern to make the app feel more calming?

TYPE THIS PROMPT

Can you show me a random entry from my past whenever I open the app, as a nice surprise?

Part Two: A Home Inventory App

A home inventory is simply a record of what you own, useful for insurance purposes, for peace of mind, or simply to remember what is in that one closet you never open. It sounds tedious to build by hand in a notebook, which is exactly why an app is such a good fit.

What You Will Build

A place to add an item with its name, the room it is in, and its estimated value

A way to group or filter items by room

A running total of estimated value for insurance purposes

A simple, organized look, similar to a checklist

Step 1: Write Your First Prompt

TYPE THIS PROMPT

Build me a simple home inventory app. It will be used just by me, on my own computer, mainly for insurance and organization purposes. I should be able to add an item with its name, the room it is in, such as Living Room or Kitchen, and its estimated value in dollars. I should be able to filter the list to show only items from one room at a time. At the top, show a running total of the estimated value of everything I have added. Please make it look organized and simple, like a clean checklist, with a neutral gray or navy color.

Step 2: Try It Out

1. Add an item, such as a television, with its room and an estimated value

2. Add a second item from a different room

3. Filter the list to show only items from one of the two rooms

4. Confirm the running total at the top reflects both items when no filter is applied

Make It Yours

TYPE THIS PROMPT

Can you add a field for the purchase date or how old the item is?

TYPE THIS PROMPT

Can you let me export or print the full list, so I have a copy saved outside the app as well?

TYPE THIS PROMPT

Can you add a note field for each item, like the serial number or where I bought it?

Saving Your Work

For both of these apps, but especially the home inventory, it is worth *asking your tool directly how to keep a backup copy* outside the app itself, such as a *downloadable file or a printed page.* Ask, "*Can you let me export this list as a simple file I can save separately?*" Your tool will show you the option available for the platform you chose.

If Something Goes Wrong

Journal entries appear in the wrong order. Say, "*Can you sort my entries so the most recent one is always at the top?*"

The room filter on the inventory app is not working. Say, "*When I choose a room from the filter, it is still showing every item. Can you fix that?*"

The running total does not match what you expect. Say, "*The total at the top does not seem to add up correctly. Can you check the math and fix it?*"

A Few Questions About These Apps

Is a gratitude journal only for people going through a hard time?

Not at all. It is simply a small daily habit that many people, in all kinds of circumstances, find quietly worthwhile. There is no requirement to be struggling in order to benefit from noticing a few good things each day. In fact, it is really the little things that can make our lives better and which often go unnoticed. A gratitude journal can help us look at our environment in a different way and begin to appreciate what's there and how it benefits us by simply noticing it.

Do I need to photograph every item for my home inventory to be useful for insurance?

A written list with estimated values is already useful on its own. If you want to go further, try the prompt, "*Can you let me attach a photo to each item in my inventory?*" and your AI tool will tell you whether that feature is available.

What if I want to keep my journal private, even from accidentally sharing my screen?

Simply keep this app in its own separate conversation or account area, away from anything you might share with others, and be mindful about which browser tab is visible when others are nearby.

Chapter Recap

You built a personal gratitude journal with dated entries

You built a bonus home inventory app with a running value total

You now have five main apps plus one bonus project, all built with the same simple method

Six apps built. That is not a small accomplishment, and it is worth pausing to notice it. In Chapter 10, you will learn how to handle moments when something does not work quite right, along with encouragement and ideas for where to take your new skills next.

Chapter 10: Fixing Mistakes and What Comes Next

You have now built six real apps. If you worked through Chapters 5 through 9 at your own pace, you already know that things did not always work on the very first try, and you already know how to fix that when it happens. This final chapter gathers everything you have learned about troubleshooting into one place, and then turns to the question every reader eventually asks: what now?

The AI Is Never Frustrated By You

Before anything else, sit with this fact for a moment, because it matters more than any technical tip in this chapter. The AI you are working with does not get tired, does not get impatient, and does not think less of you for asking the same question twice, or for not knowing the right words. You can ask it to explain something five different ways without ever wearing out its patience. There is no version of this process where you are being a bother.

The One Troubleshooting Method You Actually Need

This entire book has quietly taught you one single troubleshooting method, used over and over in slightly different clothes. Here it is, spelled out directly:

1. Notice what you expected to happen
2. Notice what actually happened instead
3. Describe both, in plain words, to your AI tool
4. Let it make the fix, and check the result

That is the whole method. It worked for adding a running total to your budget tracker in Chapter 5, and it will keep working for problems this book never specifically mentioned, because it does not depend on knowing any technical vocabulary. It only depends on paying attention to *the gap between what you wanted and what you got.*

A Longer List of Common Problems and Exact Words to Fix Them

Here is a broader troubleshooting reference you can return to any time, across any of the apps in this book, or any new app you build on your own:

Problem: Nothing happens when I click a button. Say, "*When I click this button, nothing happens. Can you check why and fix it?*"

Problem: My information disappears when I close and reopen the app. Say, "*Can you make sure everything I enter is saved so it does not disappear when I come back?*"

Problem: The app looks cluttered or hard to read. Say, "*Can you simplify the layout and make the text larger and easier to read?*"

Problem: A number is not calculating correctly. Say, "*This total does not look right. Can you check the math and fix it?*"

Problem: I want to remove a feature I no longer need. Say, "*Can you remove the [feature name], I am not using it and it is cluttering the screen.*"

Problem: I am not sure why something looks the way it does. Say, "*Can you explain in plain words why this part looks like this, with no technical terms?*"

Problem: The colors or style feel wrong for how I want to use the app. Say, "*Can you change the color scheme to something calmer or more* energetic?" whichever fits your goal.

Problem: I started over and lost my progress. Say, "*Can we go back to the last working version and continue from there?*"

WATCH OUT FOR

If a fix does not work on the first try, *resist the urge to think the tool is broken* or that you have done something wrong. Simply describe, once more and as specifically as you can, what is still not right. Two or three rounds of small adjustments are a completely normal part of building anything, *not a sign of failure.*

When to Simply Start Fresh

Occasionally, especially after many rounds of small changes, an app can start to feel tangled, with pieces that do not quite fit together the way you want. When that happens, there is *no shame in starting a new conversation and building again from a clean prompt,* using everything you have learned about what you actually want this time. Many experienced vibe coders consider this a normal part of the process, not a failure. Your second attempt at any app in this book will almost always go faster and smoother than your first, because you already know what you are asking for.

Keeping Your Apps Safe and Backed Up

As your collection of apps grows, it is worth building a simple habit of checking, every so often, that your work is actually saved somewhere you can find it again. A few simple habits go a long way:

Keep a simple note, in any document or notebook you like, listing *which tool you used for each app*, so you always know where to find it again.

If your tool offers an export, download, or share link option, *use it occasionally for the apps you care about most*, especially the home inventory app from Chapter 9.

If you are ever unsure whether something is saved, simply ask your AI tool directly, *"Is this information saved, and where can I find it if I come back later?"*

You Are Allowed to Feel Proud of This

It is worth pausing here, because it is easy to rush past this feeling. A few weeks or days ago, when you started this book, you may have believed you were not the kind of person who builds software. That belief was never true, but it can be a stubborn one. Six working apps later, built entirely in plain English, the evidence says otherwise. This is a genuine, transferable skill, and it belongs to you now, not just to the six examples in this book.

Where to Go From Here

If you have enjoyed this process, here are a few directions worth considering, *none of them required*, none of them urgent:

Build a seventh app of your own design, using the four-part formula from Chapter 4, for any small problem in your daily life.

Show a family member or friend one of your apps, and *offer to help them build their own*. Teaching it back is one of the fastest ways to feel confident in a new skill. It's also one of the best ways to reinforce the skills you have developed and to find things you may need to clarify for yourself in order to improve the knowledge you already have.

If you find yourself curious about what is happening underneath the plain English, some readers eventually explore a beginner course in traditional coding out of pure curiosity. This is entirely optional, and this book's promise stands regardless: you do not need it to keep building useful apps for your own life.

Keep an eye on the tools mentioned in Chapter 3. They *update often*, and new free features tend to make this process even easier over time, not harder.

A Final Word

Andrej Karpathy, whose words opened this book, once described handing over the typing and focusing on the idea instead. That is exactly what you have spent this book learning to do, in your own words, at your pace, for your life. There was never a technical wall between you and this skill. There was only the first prompt you hadn't typed or spoken yet. You have now typed and spoken many. *Keep going, one plain sentence at a time.*

Appendix A: The Complete Prompt Reference Card

Every prompt from this book is collected here in one place, so you never have to flip back through chapters to find one. Copy any of these directly into your AI tool's chat box, word for word, or use them as a starting point and adjust the details to fit your own life.

The Fill in the Blank Formula (Chapter 4)

TYPE THIS PROMPT

Build me a simple app that helps me [what the app is for]. It will be used by [who will use it]. When I open it, I should be able to [first thing it does], [second thing it does], and [third thing it does]. Please make it look [style or mood], with easy to read text and large buttons.

A Strong Starter Example (Chapter 4)

TYPE THIS PROMPT

Build me a simple to-do list app that helps me keep track of errands during the week. It will be used just by me. When I open it, I should be able to type in a new errand and add it to the list, check a box next to an errand once it is done, and clear away the finished errands with one button. Please make it look clean and simple, with large text and a soft blue color.

The Universal Fix-It Message (Chapter 4)

TYPE THIS PROMPT

This is not quite right. I expected [what you expected] but instead [what actually happened]. Can you fix that?

Chapter 5: Personal Budget Tracker

Starting Prompt

TYPE THIS PROMPT

Build me a simple personal budget tracker app. It will be used just by me, on my own computer. When I open it, I should be able to type in my total income for the month at the top.

Below that, I should be able to add expenses one at a time, each with a short name, a dollar amount, and a category like Housing, Food, Transportation, or Fun. As I add expenses, show a running total of how much I have spent so far and a clear number showing how much of my income is left. Please make it look clean and calm, with a soft green color, large readable text, and simple buttons.

Make It Yours

TYPE THIS PROMPT

Can you add a pie chart or simple bar chart that shows how much I am spending in each category?

TYPE THIS PROMPT

Can you let me mark an expense as recurring, so I do not have to type it in again next month?

TYPE THIS PROMPT

Can you change the categories to Housing, Food, Transportation, Insurance, and Savings to match how I actually organize my money?

TYPE THIS PROMPT

Can you add a small note at the top that turns red if my expenses go over my income?

TYPE THIS PROMPT

Can you make the text and buttons a little larger so they are easier to read?

Chapter 6: Daily Habit Tracker
Starting Prompt

TYPE THIS PROMPT

Build me a simple daily habit tracker app. It will be used just by me, on my own computer. I should be able to type in a list of habits I want to track, such as Drink Water, Take a Walk, and Read for Ten Minutes. For each habit, show a row of seven checkboxes, one for each day of the week. Let me check off a day once I complete that habit. Next to each habit, show a small streak counter that counts how many days in a row I have checked it off. Please make it look warm and encouraging, with a soft yellow or orange color and large, friendly text.

Make It Yours

TYPE THIS PROMPT

Can you let me add a new habit whenever I want, using a small add button, instead of only at the start?

TYPE THIS PROMPT

Can you add a short encouraging message that appears once I check off all my habits for the day, like "Great job today?"

TYPE THIS PROMPT

Can you change the week to start on Monday instead of Sunday?

TYPE THIS PROMPT

Can you add a way to remove a habit I am no longer tracking?

TYPE THIS PROMPT

Can you show my longest ever streak next to my current streak, so I can see my personal best?

Chapter 7: Family Calendar and Chore Chart
Starting Prompt

TYPE THIS PROMPT

Build me a simple family calendar and chore chart app. It will be used by everyone in my household. When I open it, I should see a weekly view with a column for each day, Monday through Sunday. I should be able to add a chore, type in who it is assigned to, and pick which day it is due. Each chore should have a checkbox to mark it done. Please make it look bright and friendly, easy for both adults and kids to read, with clear day labels at the top of each column.

Make It Yours

TYPE THIS PROMPT

Can you add a different color for each family member's name, so it is easy to tell at a glance whose chores are whose?

TYPE THIS PROMPT

Can you add a way to mark a chore as repeating every week, so I do not have to add it again next week?

TYPE THIS PROMPT

Can you add a small section at the top for family events or appointments, separate from the daily chores?

TYPE THIS PROMPT

Can you make the finished chores move to the bottom of the list instead of just changing color, so the unfinished ones are easier to spot?

TYPE THIS PROMPT

Can you add a simple weekly summary at the bottom showing how many chores each person completed?

Chapter 8: Recipe Box and Meal Planner

Starting Prompt

TYPE THIS PROMPT

Build me a simple recipe box and weekly meal planner app. It will be used just by me and my family on our own computer. I should be able to add a new recipe with a name, a list of ingredients, and short cooking instructions. I should be able to see all my saved recipes in a list and click on one to see its full details. Below that, show a weekly meal planner with a slot for each day of the week, where I can pick one of my saved recipes to plan for that day. Please make it look warm and homey, with a cream or light orange color and easy-to-read text.

Make It Yours

TYPE THIS PROMPT

Can you add a way to tag each recipe as breakfast, lunch, dinner, or snack, and let me filter my list by that tag?

TYPE THIS PROMPT

Can you automatically create a combined grocery list from whatever recipes I have planned for the week?

TYPE THIS PROMPT

Can you add a small note field on each recipe where I can write things like "my mother-in-law's version" or "add extra garlic"?

TYPE THIS PROMPT

Can you let me mark a recipe as a favorite and show favorites at the top of the list?

TYPE THIS PROMPT

Can you add a search box at the top so I can quickly find a recipe by name or ingredient?

Chapter 9: Gratitude Journal

Starting Prompt

TYPE THIS PROMPT

Build me a simple gratitude journal app. It will be used just by me, on my own computer. Each day, I should be able to type in a few things I am grateful for and save the entry with today's date attached automatically. I should be able to scroll back through my past entries, sorted with the most recent one at the top. Please make it look calm and gentle, with a soft lavender or pale blue color, and simple, uncluttered text.

Make It Yours

TYPE THIS PROMPT

Can you add a gentle prompt or question each day, like what made you smile today, to help me get started writing?

TYPE THIS PROMPT

Can you let me look back at entries from a specific month, instead of scrolling through everything?

TYPE THIS PROMPT

Can you add a soft background image or simple pattern to make the app feel more calming?

TYPE THIS PROMPT

Can you show me a random entry from my past whenever I open the app, as a nice surprise?

Chapter 9 Bonus: Home Inventory App
Starting Prompt

TYPE THIS PROMPT

Build me a simple home inventory app. It will be used just by me, on my own computer, mainly for insurance and organization purposes. I should be able to add an item with its name, the room it is in, such as Living Room or Kitchen, and its estimated value in dollars. I should be able to filter the list to show only items from one room at a time. At the top, show a running total of the estimated value of everything I have added. Please make it look organized and simple, like a clean checklist, with a neutral gray or navy color.

Make It Yours

TYPE THIS PROMPT

Can you add a field for the purchase date or how old the item is?

TYPE THIS PROMPT

Can you let me export or print the full list, so I have a copy saved outside the app as well?

TYPE THIS PROMPT

Can you add a note field for each item, like the serial number or where I bought it?

Appendix B: Glossary of Words You Need to Know

This book promised no jargon, and it has kept that promise throughout. Still, a small number of everyday words come up again and again, so here they all are in one place, defined once, in plain language, for whenever you want to double-check one.

Account

A free profile you create with an email address so a website can remember your work between visits.

Agent

A more independent AI tool that can carry out several steps on its own, such as building and testing an app, before showing you the result. *Replit's Agent feature* is one example mentioned in this book.

AI

Short for artificial intelligence. A computer program built to understand language, answer questions, and, in this book's case, write software based on a plain English description.

AI coding assistant

A website or tool, like Claude or ChatGPT, that can write working software from a plain English description.

API

Short for application programming interface. A technical way for two pieces of software to talk to each other. You will not need to work with this interface directly for anything in this book.

App

Short for application. A program on your computer, tablet, or phone that does one job well, such as tracking your budget or your habits.

Artifact

The name Claude uses for a working app or piece of content it builds and shows you directly inside the chat window.

Backup

A separate, saved copy of your work, kept in case something happens to the original.

Beta

A word used for a tool or feature that is still being tested and improved. New AI features are sometimes labeled this way.

Browser

The program you use to look at websites, such as Chrome, Safari, or Edge. Every tool in this book runs inside a browser.

Bug

A small mistake in how an app behaves, such as a button that does not work. Easily fixed by describing the problem in plain words.

Cache, or history

The record of your past conversations is kept by a tool, which allows you to return to an app you built previously.

Chat box

The text box on screen where you type your messages, or prompts, to an AI tool.

Chatbot

Another common name for an AI tool you talk to using typed messages, such as ChatGPT or Claude.

Cloud

A general term for information stored on the internet or on someone else's computer, rather than only on your own device.

Code, or computer code

The exact, technical instructions that make software run. In vibe coding, the AI writes the code for you, and you never need to read or understand it.

Credits, or tokens

A way some free tools measure how much building you can do before you hit a daily or monthly limit

Cursor, the tool

A separate AI coding tool, mentioned briefly in this book, is designed more for people who already write some code themselves.

Data

Any information stored by an app, such as your list of expenses or your saved recipes.

Debugging

The traditional programming term for finding and fixing a bug. In this book, debugging simply means describing what looks wrong to your AI tool.

Deploy, or publish

Making an app available to use outside of just your chat window, sometimes as a shareable web link.

Dictation

Speaking out loud instead of typing, using your device's built-in microphone feature, supported by most modern browsers and devices.

Domain

The address of a website, such as claude.ai or replit.com.

Download

Saving a copy of a file from a website onto your own device.

Export

Saving a copy of your app or its information *in a separate file, outside the tool itself*, so you always have a backup.

Feature

Any single thing an app can do, such as a running total, a streak counter, or a search box.

Free tier

The version of a tool that costs nothing to use, usually with some daily or monthly limits.

Free trial

A limited time or limited use offer that eventually requires payment, different from a true ongoing free tier. This book relies solely on true free tiers.

Interface, or screen

The part of an app you actually see and interact with, including its buttons, text boxes, and colors.

Iteration

Making a small improvement and checking the result, then repeating. This is the normal rhythm of building any app in this book.

Large language model (LLM)

The technical name for the kind of AI, such as the ones behind Claude and ChatGPT, that can understand and respond to plain English and produce working computer code.

Login, or sign in

Entering your email and password, or a similar method, to access your existing account on a website.

Notification

A small alert or message a tool shows you, such as confirming that your work has been saved.

Placeholder

Example or made-up information used to test an app, such as a fake name or a round number, instead of real personal details.

Preview

A working, clickable version of an app shown to you before or without formally publishing it.

Prompt

The message you type to an AI tool describing what you want it to build or change.

Responsive design

A way of building an app so it looks good and works well on both a large computer screen and a small phone screen.

Sandbox

A safe, closed-off space where an app can run and be tested without any chance of it affecting your real computer or files.

Save

Keeping a copy of your work so it is available the next time you open the app or return to your conversation.

Server

A computer, owned and run by a company like *Anthropic or OpenAI,* that does the actual work of building and running your app, rather than your device.

Session

A single sitting of using a tool, from opening it to closing it.

Share link

A web address that lets someone else open and use an app you built without needing an account of their own.

Sign up

Creating a brand new account on a website for the first time, usually with an email address.

Software

Another word for a computer program, including every app built in this book.

Streak

A count of how many days in a row you have kept up a habit, as used in the habit tracker from Chapter 6.

Template

A ready-made starting point for an app or document that you can adjust to fit your needs.

Version

A particular saved state of your app at a specific point in time. Some tools let you look back at earlier versions if a recent change did not work out.

Vibe coding

Describing what you want in plain, everyday language and letting an AI tool write the computer code, rather than writing the code yourself.

Vibe engineering

A term some professional engineers use for a more careful, reviewed version of vibe coding used on serious, high-stakes software. Not something a beginner needs to worry about for the personal apps in this book.

Web app

An app that runs inside a web browser, rather than one you download and install separately. Every app in this book is a web app.

Appendix C: Notes and Sources

This book leans on real, respected voices from the software world rather than guesswork, so that the reassurance it offers you is backed by people who genuinely know this field. Here is where each idea came from, *along with where you can read more in their own words if you would like to.*

Andrej Karpathy

Andrej Karpathy is a computer scientist and one of the founding members of OpenAI, the company behind ChatGPT, and he has also held a senior AI leadership role at Tesla. In February 2025, he posted a short message describing a new style of working, where a person describes what they want in plain language and lets an AI handle the actual typing of the code. He named this vibe coding, and the term spread quickly through the technology world and beyond, eventually becoming common enough to appear in mainstream news coverage and even reference works like Wikipedia.

Where to read his original words:

Andrej Karpathy's original post on vibe coding (X, formerly Twitter)

Simon Willison

Simon Willison is a software engineer and writer well known in the technology world for creating widely used open source tools, including Django and Datasette, and for his detailed, careful public writing on AI and software. He has been especially thoughtful about the responsible side of vibe coding, drawing a clear line between building something you have tested and understood versus accepting AI-generated work blindly. His writing on the topic informed this book's emphasis on always trying out what you build and always speaking up when something does not match what you expected.

Where to read more of his writing:

Not all AI-assisted programming is vibe coding, by Simon Willison

Gene Kim and Steve Yegge

Gene Kim is a widely read author on how modern organizations build software, known for books including *The Phoenix Project* and *The DevOps Handbook*. Steve Yegge is a veteran software engineer who has worked at some of the largest technology companies in the world. Together they wrote a full-length book for professional software teams on building production software with AI assistance, which won a major industry book award in 2026. Their work is referenced in this book as evidence that vibe coding is being taken seriously by experienced professionals, not treated as a shortcut or a fad.

Where to find their book:

Vibe Coding: Building Production-Grade Software with GenAI, Chat, Agents, and Beyond, by Gene Kim and Steve Yegge

MIT Technology Review

For a clear, independent journalistic explanation of what vibe coding is and how it is being used and discussed across the technology industry, this book drew on coverage from MIT Technology Review, a publication produced by the Massachusetts Institute of Technology and widely respected for its reporting on emerging technology.

Where to read it:

What is vibe coding, exactly? MIT Technology Review: A search on Google will give you the correct URL for this article.

A General Reference

For a broad, regularly updated overview of the term, its history, and how it is used, Wikipedia's entry on vibe coding is a reasonable starting point for further reading.

Vibe coding, Wikipedia

On the Free Tools Mentioned in Chapter 3

Details about free tiers, features, and sign-up steps for the tools in Chapter 3 change from time to time, since these are actively developed products. This book describes them accurately as of its writing, but it is always worth checking each tool's own website for its current terms, pricing, and features before you sign up.

- **Claude, by Anthropic: claude.ai**
- **ChatGPT, by OpenAI: chatgpt.com**
- **Replit: replit.com**
- **Bolt.new, by StackBlitz: bolt.new**
- **Lovable: lovable.dev**

Appendix D: Frequently Asked Questions

This appendix gathers honest questions that beginners commonly ask, along with plain, direct answers. If you have a concern, and it's not listed here, remember that you can always *ask your AI tool* the same question directly, in your own words.

Will this cost me any money?

No. Every tool recommended in this book has a free tier that is more than enough to build all six apps in this book. Some tools place a daily or monthly limit on free use, covered in Chapter 3, but none require payment to get started or to use the apps you build on an ongoing basis.

Is my personal information safe when I use these tools?

Treat any AI chat box the way you would treat a conversation with a helpful stranger. *Avoid typing real passwords, full account numbers, or sensitive medical or government identification numbers,* even as an example. Use placeholder information instead when practicing, and read a tool's own privacy information if you plan to store genuinely personal data in an app long term.

Do I need the internet every time I want to use my app?

Yes, for the tools in this book, since they run inside a web browser and are built and hosted online. This is what allows them to be free and to require no installation. If you want an app that works fully offline, that is a more advanced project outside the scope of this book.

Can I use these apps on my phone, not just my computer?

In most cases, yes. Since these apps run in a web browser, you can typically open the same link or account on your phone's browser. Tools like Replit, in particular, are built with this kind of access in mind. If you want an app that behaves more like a traditional phone app with its own icon, *ask your AI tool directly* whether that is possible with the platform you chose.

What happens if the AI tool I am using shuts down or changes?

This is a fair concern, since technology companies do change their products over time. The skill you are building in this book, describing what you want clearly and iterating on the result, transfers directly to any future tool. If one tool changes in a way you don't like, you can rebuild the same app in a different free tool from Chapter 3 using the very same prompts from Appendix A.

Am I actually learning to code or just using a shortcut?

You are learning a genuinely useful, transferable skill: describing software clearly enough for it to be built correctly. That is not a lesser skill than traditional coding, *it is a different one*, and as Chapter 2 explained, respected professional engineers are using and studying this same approach in their own serious work.

Should I eventually learn traditional coding too?

Only if you want to, out of curiosity or for a specific goal like a career change. Nothing in this book requires it, and you can keep building useful, personal apps for the rest of your life using only the method taught here.

Can I sell an app I build this way?

Some people do go on to build and sell simple apps or websites using these same tools, but this book is focused on building apps for your own personal use. If you become interested in selling software you build, *look into each tool's terms of service* regarding ownership and commercial use before doing so.

What if I do not have a specific app idea from this book in mind?

Start with whichever of the six apps in Chapters 5 through 9 sounds most useful to your own life right now. There is no required order beyond reading the foundational Chapters 1 through 4 first.

Is it normal to need many attempts before an app feels right?

Completely normal and expected. Every app in this book is described as being built through a back-and-forth conversation, not a single perfect request. Chapter 10 covers this in detail.

What if I do not understand a word the AI uses in its response?

Simply ask. A message as plain as "Can you explain that without any technical words?" will get you a plain language answer every time. The AI is not limited to using jargon, it simply sometimes falls into old habits, and a quick request will reset that.

Can I build an app for something not covered in this book?

Yes, and you are encouraged to. The four-part prompt formula in Chapter 4 and the troubleshooting method in Chapter 10 work for any small, personal app idea, not only the six covered here.

Do I need to know which AI tool is the newest or most powerful?

No. New tools and updates arrive constantly in this field, and trying to track all of them is unnecessary for the goals of this book. Any of the free tools in Chapter 3 will comfortably handle every project here.

For example, Claude will include a small note, usually in the lower left-hand corner, that will tell you an update is available.

What if my grandchildren or a younger family member want to help me?

Wonderful, invite them. Many readers find it enjoyable to build a first app together with a younger family member, since the plain language approach in this book makes it easy for people of very different technical backgrounds to collaborate on the same project. This can actually be a fun family project or even a social interaction activity for a small group of friends or neighbors. You might want to write or build an app for a block security system, and who might be responsible for that and how would that be accomplished? This is just an additional idea, not an indication that you should go off and build that app.

Will my apps look as polished as ones made by professional companies?

They will look clean, functional, and genuinely usable, especially once you have gone through a few rounds of the "Make It Yours" **prompts in each chapter.** They are built for your own personal use, not for a store shelf, so professional-level polish is not the goal, usefulness is.

What if I get an error message I do not understand?

Copy or describe the error message as best you can, and simply paste or describe it back to your AI tool along with the phrase, "*I got this message. Can you explain what it means and fix* it?" This works even if you can't make sense of the message yourself.

Can more than one person edit the same app?

The answer depends on the specific tool and is most naturally supported by tools like Lovable and Replit, which are built with shared, ongoing projects in mind. Ask your tool directly, "*Can more than one person work on this app?*" for the most current answer.

How do I know which free tool is truly the best one?

There is no single correct answer, and Chapter 3 deliberately avoids declaring one winner. The best tool is the one you actually open and use. All five recommended tools are fully capable of building every app in this book.

What if I want to stop and come back to this book later?

That is completely fine. Each chapter stands on its own once you have read Chapters 1 through 4, and your apps remain saved in your account's history whenever you are ready to pick the process back up.

Is there a wrong way to describe what I want?

No. Plain, everyday language is the entire point of this method. There is no required format, no penalty for imperfect grammar, and no way to phrase a request so poorly that it cannot simply be clarified with a follow-up message.

What computer or tablet do I actually need?

Any laptop, desktop, or tablet from roughly the last several years that can open a modern web browser, such as Chrome, Safari, or Edge, is enough. You don't need a fast processor, a large amount of storage, or any special graphics capability, since the actual building happens on the tool's own servers, not on your device.

Do I need to type quickly or accurately to do this well?

No. Many readers of this book type slowly, and some tools let you speak your prompt out loud instead of typing it, using your device's built-in dictation feature. What matters is the clarity of the idea, not the speed or polish of the typing. The author of this book dictates with *Wispr Flow software*.

What if English is not my first language?

AI tools are generally quite good at understanding plain language even with non-native phrasing, spelling mistakes, or grammar that is not perfectly formal. Focus on getting your idea across as clearly as you can, in whichever way feels most natural to you.

Can I use these tools if I have trouble seeing small text?

Every tool in Chapter 3 also lets you zoom in on your web browser, the same way you can on any website, to make everything larger and easier to read.

What if I only have thirty minutes here and there to work on this?

That is genuinely enough time. Every app in this book can be started, and often finished, in a single thirty-minute sitting. Longer projects, like fully customizing an app with every optional feature, can simply be spread across several short sessions.

Will I need to remember complicated menus or settings?

No. Almost everything in this book happens through the plain text chat box. A small number of buttons, like "sign up" or "create new," are the only clicking involved, and this book tells you exactly where to find them. Keep in mind that the AI app is sitting there and waiting for any questions you may have. This means ANY questions. Don't hesitate if you don't understand something. Ask for it to be explained again or rephrased until you are comfortable and do understand what was provided.

What if two of my apps could work well together, like the budget tracker and the recipe box?

You can absolutely ask for that. Try a prompt like, "*Can you connect my grocery list from the meal planner to a new expense in my budget tracker*?" Whether it can be done in a single step depends on your specific tool, but it is a reasonable thing to ask for.

Is it safe to leave my apps running or open all the time?

Yes. These are simple, personal tools with no unusual behavior in the background. Treat them the same way you would treat any other browser tab or website you keep open.

What if I want a version of an app for a different member of my family, separately from mine?

The simplest approach is to build a fresh copy in a new conversation *for each person*, so everyone has their own independent version. Some tools also support separate accounts entirely, which your AI tool can explain if you ask directly.

Do I need to tell the AI that I am a beginner?

It rarely hurts, and it can help. Many readers find it useful to open a new project with a short line like, "*Please explain things in plain, simple language, I am new to this.*" Most AI tools will happily adjust their style based on that request.

What if I want to build something more ambitious later, beyond a personal app?

The same core skill, describing what you want clearly and iterating on the result, scales up to larger projects too. Larger projects typically involve more planning and more back and forth, but the fundamental method taught in this book does not change.

Can I lose work I have already built if my internet goes out mid-session?

Most tools save your progress continuously as you go, but it is a reasonable habit to avoid making a large batch of changes right before you know your connection may drop. If you are ever unsure, ***ask your tool directly***, "*Is my recent work saved?*" before closing your browser.

What if I disagree with a change the AI made, even after asking for it?

You are always allowed to change your mind. Simply say, "*Actually, can you undo that last* change?" or describe what you would prefer instead. There is no obligation to keep a change just because you already asked for it once.

Appendix E: 10 More App Ideas to Try Next

If you have finished the six apps in this book and are hungry for more practice, here are ten additional ideas, each with a *ready to use starting prompt.* Use the same method from every chapter: send the prompt, look at what comes back, and describe any changes you would like in plain words.

A Bill Payment Reminder

A simple place to list your recurring bills, their due dates, and whether each one has been paid this month, so nothing slips through the cracks.

TYPE THIS PROMPT

Build me a simple bill payment reminder app. It will be used just by me. I should be able to add a bill with its name, due

date, and amount and mark it as paid once I have taken care of it. Please show unpaid bills at the top, sorted by due date, and make it look clean and simple with a calming blue color.

A Packing List Generator

A tool that keeps a reusable packing list for trips, so you are not rewriting the same list from memory every time you travel.

TYPE THIS PROMPT

Build me a simple packing list app. It will be used just by me before trips. I should be able to create a new list, add items to it with checkboxes, and mark items as packed. Let me save a list as a template I can reuse for future trips. Please make it look clean and organized, with a soft teal color.

A Reading List Tracker

A place to track books you want to read, books you are currently reading, and books you have finished, along with a simple rating.

TYPE THIS PROMPT

Build me a simple reading list app. It will be used just by me. I should be able to add a book with its title and author and mark it as want to read, currently reading, or finished. For finished

books, let me give it a star rating from one to five. Please make it look cozy and simple, with a warm cream background.

A Garden Planner

A seasonal planner for what to plant, when to plant it, and when to expect a harvest, useful for anyone who keeps a vegetable garden or flower beds.

TYPE THIS PROMPT

Build me a simple garden planner app. It will be used just by me. I should be able to add a plant with its name, the month I plan to plant it, and the month I expect to harvest it. Show the plants grouped by planting month. Please make it look fresh and natural, with a green color scheme.

A Pet Care Schedule

A shared record of feeding times, walks, and vet appointments for a family pet, especially useful in a household where more than one person shares pet duties.

TYPE THIS PROMPT

Build me a simple pet care schedule app. It will be used by my whole household. I should be able to log a feeding, a walk, or a vet visit with the date and who did it. Show today's log at the

top, and let me see a simple history below it. Please make it look friendly and bright, with a soft yellow color.

A Gift and Birthday Tracker

A place to remember birthdays, anniversaries, and gift ideas for the people in your life, so you are never caught off guard.

TYPE THIS PROMPT

Build me a simple gift and birthday tracker app. It will be used just by me. I should be able to add a person's name, their birthday or anniversary date, and a running list of gift ideas for them. Show upcoming dates in the next thirty days at the top. Please make it look warm and personal, with a soft pink or coral color.

A Simple Workout Log

A basic record of workouts, useful for noticing patterns and progress over time without needing a complicated fitness app.

TYPE THIS PROMPT

Build me a simple workout log app. It will be used just by me. I should be able to log a workout with the date, the type of activity, and how long it lasted. Show my recent workouts in a list, most recent first, and show a simple weekly total of minutes

exercised. Please make it look energetic but clean, with a bold blue or orange color.

A Car Maintenance Log

A record of oil changes, tire rotations, and other car maintenance, so you always know what was done and when.

TYPE THIS PROMPT

Build me a simple car maintenance log app. It will be used just by me. I should be able to log a service with the date, the type of service such as oil change or tire rotation, and the mileage at the time. Show my service history sorted by most recent date first. Please make it look simple and practical, with a dark gray and silver color scheme.

A Party Guest List and RSVP Tracker

A simple way to track who you have invited to an event and whether they have responded, instead of juggling texts and a paper list.

TYPE THIS PROMPT

Build me a simple guest list and RSVP tracker app. It will be used just by me while planning an event. I should be able to add a guest's name and mark their RSVP status as invited, yes, no, or no response yet. Show a simple count at the top of how many

have said yes. Please make it look festive but easy to read, with a soft purple color.

A Simple Personal Notes Board

A catch-all space for quick notes, reminders, and ideas that do not fit neatly into any of the other apps in this book.

TYPE THIS PROMPT

Build me a simple personal notes app. It will be used just by me. I should be able to add a short note and see all my notes displayed like sticky notes on a board. Let me delete a note once I no longer need it. Please make it look playful and simple, with a few different soft pastel colors for variety.

A Water Intake Tracker

A simple daily counter for how many glasses of water you have had, with a gentle visual goal to work toward.

TYPE THIS PROMPT

Build me a simple water intake tracker app. It will be used just by me. I should be able to tap a button each time I drink a glass of water and see a running count for today, along with a simple progress bar toward a daily goal of eight glasses. Let me change

my daily goal if I want to. Please make it look refreshing, with a light blue color.

A Simple Contact and Important Numbers List

A single, organized place for phone numbers you reach for often, like family members, doctors, and utility companies.

TYPE THIS PROMPT

Build me a simple contact list app. It will be used just by me, for important phone numbers. I should be able to add a contact with their name, phone number, and a category such as Family, Medical, or Utilities. Let me filter the list by category. Please make it look clean and easy to scan quickly, with large text.

A Moving or Decluttering Checklist

A room-by-room checklist for a move or a big decluttering project so nothing gets forgotten in the process.

TYPE THIS PROMPT

Build me a simple moving and decluttering checklist app. It will be used just by me. I should be able to add a room, and under each room add tasks or items with a checkbox. Show a simple overall percentage complete at the top. Please make

it look organized and calm, with a soft gray and white color scheme.

A Simple Mood Log

A brief, private daily check-in on how you are feeling is useful for noticing patterns over weeks or months.

TYPE THIS PROMPT

Build me a simple daily mood log app. It will be used just by me. Each day, I should be able to pick a mood from a short list, such as great, good, okay, or tough, and add an optional short note. Let me look back through past days in a simple list. Please make it look gentle and non-judgmental, with a soft neutral color scheme.

Appendix F: 30-Day Vibe Coding Practice Plan

You don't need a plan to succeed with this book, and you are welcome to move at whatever pace suits you. But if a simple day-by-day structure would help, here is one path through everything in this book, spread across thirty days, with room to rest along the way. Feel free to move faster, slower, or out of order. There is no wrong pace.

Day 1

Create your free account with the tool you chose in Chapter 3, and send it one simple, friendly hello message just to see how it responds.

Day 2

Write and send your very first prompt using the four-part formula from Chapter 4 for any small idea of your own.

Day 3

Build the personal budget tracker from Chapter 5, using the starting prompt in Appendix A.

Day 4

Test your budget tracker with a full week of real or sample expenses.

Day 5

Send one "make it yours" prompt to your budget tracker, chosen from Chapter 5 or Appendix A.

Day 6

Rest. Simply reread Chapter 2 and notice how much more familiar the ideas already feel.

Day 7

Build the daily habit tracker from Chapter 6, and add three real habits you want to build.

Day 8

Check in on your habit tracker and mark today's progress.

Day 9

Send a "make it yours" prompt to your habit tracker.

Day 10

Build the family calendar and chore chart from Chapter 7, with real chores and real names.

Day 11

Show your family calendar to at least one other member of your household, and ask what they would change.

Day 12

Send a "make it yours" prompt to your family calendar based on that feedback.

Day 13

Rest. Reread the troubleshooting method in Chapter 10, even though you may not need it yet.

Day 14

Build the recipe box from Chapter 8, and add two recipes you actually cook.

Day 15

Add two more recipes to your recipe box, for a total of at least four.

Day 16

Build the meal planner half of Chapter 8 and plan out one real week of meals.

Day 17

Ask your recipe app for an automatically generated grocery list, using the make it yours prompt from Chapter 8.

Day 18

Build the gratitude journal from Chapter 9, and write your first real entry.

Day 19

Write a second gratitude journal entry, on a different day, and scroll back to compare.

Day 20

Rest. Look back through everything you have built so far, and notice how far you have come in under three weeks.

Day 21

Build the bonus home inventory app from Chapter 9, and add five real items from one room in your home.

Day 22

Add items from a second room to your home inventory app.

Day 23

Ask your *home inventory app* for a way to export or print your list, using the make it yours prompt from Chapter 9.

Day 24

Pick one app you have built so far and give it a second round of improvements, describing anything that still bothers you about it.

Day 25

Try one new app idea from Appendix E, using its ready-to-use starting prompt.

Day 26

Continue customizing yesterday's new app with at least one "make it yours" prompt of your own design.

Day 27

Teach someone else, even briefly, how one of your apps works. Notice how much you already understand well enough to explain.

Day 28

Reread Appendix D, the frequently asked questions, and see how many you could now answer yourself, from experience.

Day 29

Try a second new idea from Appendix E, or invent one entirely of your own using the four-part formula.

Day 30

Look back at all six main apps plus anything extra you built, and simply notice, in writing if you like, what you are proudest of.

Appendix G: Worksheets and Notes Pages

These pages are meant to be written on or printed out, whether you print this book or simply keep your own copy of these worksheets nearby. There is no wrong way to fill them in. Printing them out would probably be more effective, since you could post them somewhere you can see them instead of calling them up on your computer. Plus, printing will give you more space, and this form doesn't do that in this book.

My Own App Worksheet

Use this page any time you want to plan a new app idea, using the four part formula from Chapter 4.

What is this app for?

Who will use it?

What should it do, step by step?

What should it look like?

My Own App Worksheet

Use this page any time you want to plan a new app idea, using the four-part formula from Chapter 4.

What is this app for?

Who will use it?

What should it do, step by step?

My App Log

Use this table to keep track of every app you build, which free tool you used, and any notes for next time.

App Name	Tool Used	Date Started	Notes

Notes

Notes

Notes

More Notes

Ideas for Apps I Want to Build Someday

Questions I Want to Ask My AI Tool Next Time

Recipes I Want to Add to My Recipe Box

Rooms and Items Still Left to Add to My Home Inventory

Habits I Want to Track Next

People I Want to Show My Apps To

My Own Notes on What I Learned

A Blank Page for Whatever You Need

Appendix H: Quick Start Checklist

Keep this page handy as a fast, at-a-glance reminder of the entire process taught in this book, from a blank screen to a finished app.

Before You Begin

- A computer or tablet with an internet connection
  - An email address for a free account
  - One free tool chosen from Chapter 3

Every Time You Build Something New

- Describe what it is for, who will use it, what it should do step-by-step, and what it should look like
  - Send your prompt and look closely at what comes back
  - Try the app yourself with a few sample entries

- Describe anything that looks different from what you expected
- Repeat the last two steps until it feels right
- Check that your work is saved before you close the tab

The Six Apps, at a Glance

Personal Budget Tracker (Chapter 5)

See income, expenses, and what is left over at a glance.

Daily Habit Tracker (Chapter 6)

Check off habits each day and watch your streaks grow.

Family Calendar and Chore Chart (Chapter 7)

One shared view of who is doing what, all week long.

Recipe Box and Meal Planner (Chapter 8)

Store your go-to recipes and plan your week around them.

Gratitude Journal (Chapter 9)

A few quiet minutes each day to notice the good things.

Home Inventory (Chapter 9 Bonus)

A simple record of your belongings, useful for insurance.

If You Get Stuck

Return to the troubleshooting method in Chapter 10: notice what you expected, notice what happened instead, describe both in plain words, and let the AI make the fix.

Appendix I: You and the Bigger AI Story

It's worth stepping back now that you have actually built something and looking again at the bigger story running in the background of daily life right now. Artificial intelligence is discussed constantly, often in sweeping, dramatic language. It is called a storm, a revolution, a force that is taking over. That kind of language can make a person feel like a bystander, watching something enormous happen far away from their kitchen table. It can also be very intimidating and make you less likely to engage with AI in a practical, personal way, as we have done here.

This book aims to provide you with a different experience of that same technology. Not as something happening to you, but as something you can pick up and use, on your own terms, for your own small, specific, personal purposes. A budget tracker. A chore chart. A journal. These are not headline-grabbing achievements, and they were never meant to be. They are proof, in your own hands, that the tools behind the big dramatic headlines are also simply useful, approachable, everyday tools, available to you exactly as they are to anyone else.

You Do Not Have to Pick a Side

Public conversation about AI often gets framed as a choice between two extremes, either wholehearted excitement or complete rejection. You do not have to choose either one. You are allowed to feel two things at once: a healthy amount of caution about a powerful new technology and a genuine, practical appreciation for a free tool that just helped you build something useful for your life. Both of those reactions are reasonable, and neither one cancels out the other.

What You Actually Gained

Set aside the bigger headlines for a moment, and consider what you concretely gained by working through this book:

- A working understanding of what AI tools can and cannot do, built from direct experience rather than secondhand opinions
- A repeatable method for describing what you want clearly enough for a computer, or another person, to understand
- Several real, useful apps, built for your life, that didn't exist before you sat down with this book
- The knowledge, now proven rather than assumed, that you were never too old, too far behind, or too unfamiliar with computers to take part in this

A Closing Thought

The people writing headlines about AI taking over rarely stop to picture someone like you, sitting at your kitchen table, quietly building a habit tracker to help you and your spouse take an evening walk together. That is a smaller, quieter story than the ones making the news. It is also, in a very real sense, the truer one, and *it is entirely yours.*

Appendix J: A Certificate, For You

Certificate of Completion

This certifies that

has read ***Vibe Coding for the Rest of Us*** and built real, working apps using nothing but plain English and free AI tools, with no coding experience required.

Write in the date you finish, and keep this page as your proof of what you built.

About the Author

Dr. Patricia A. Farrell is a licensed psychologist, published author of multiple self-help books and videos, former WebMD psychologist expert/consultant, former medical consultant for Social Security Disability Determinations, National Monitor for the first medication for Alzheimer's disease and formeer psychiatric researcher at Mt. Sinai Medical Center (NYC) and an educator who has taught at the college as well as graduate and postgraduate levels; and a top health writer for Medium.com publications. She has over four decades of experience in the field of mental health.

Dr. Farrell is a consultant to pharmaceutical firms, writes continuing education modules for mental healthcare professionals, has contributed to USMLE medical school prep courses and blogs on M edium.com and on Patreon "Dr. Farrell Unplugged," has a YouTube channel with helpful tips on multiple topics and is a biographee in Who's Who in the World, Who's Who in America and Who's Who in American Women.

A member of The American Psychological Association as well as the SAG-AFTRA union, Dr. Farrell is a former board member of the NJ Board of Psychological Examiners, a former psychiatry preceptor at UMDNJ and a former board of directors member of Bergen Pines Hospital.

Amazon author page: https://tinyurl.com/yc3vff2n
Author book links: books2read.com/drpatriciafarrell
Booksellers: https://books2read.com/drpatriciafarrell

A Special Request

If this book has touched your heart, sparked your curiosity, or simply entertained you along the way, I'd be incredibly grateful if you could take a moment to share your thoughts with a review on Amazon or wherever you discovered this book. Your words not only help other readers find books they'll love, but they also mean the world to authors like me who pour their hearts into every page. Thank you for being part of this journey and for helping books find their way to the readers who need them most.

Author Page on Amazon: ***https://tinyurl.com/zbrb6c9n*** and on Draft2Digital: ***https://tinyurl.com/mwta4w46***

Author Page on Draft2Digital: https://books2read.com/drpatriciafarrell

www.ingramcontent.com/pod-product-compliance
Lightning Source LLC
LaVergne TN
LVHW030726061126
851857LV00019B/2018
* 9 7 9 8 9 5 1 0 7 4 1 5 7 *